C000115447

HENLEY ON THAMES
A Pictorial History

The town hall, 1826.

HENLEY ON THAMES
A Pictorial History

Ann Cottingham
and
Hilary Fisher

Phillimore

1990

Published by
PHILLIMORE & CO. LTD.
Shopwyke Hall, Chichester, Sussex

© Ann Cottingham and Hilary Fisher, 1990

ISBN 0 85033 731 3

Printed and bound in Great Britain by
BIDDLES LTD.
Guildford, Surrey

List of Illustrations

Illustration Acknowledgements

We wish to thank the following people for allowing us to borrow their photographs and postcards, and for permission to reproduce them. Unfortunately, space prevents us from making use of all the pictures loaned to us.

Mr. P. Anderson, 1; Mr. J. F. Bailey, 145, 171; Mrs. Ball; Berkshire Library and Information Service, 2; Mrs. Brakspear, 155; Mr. G. Broad, 131, 134, 139, 173, 176; Mr. J. Brosnan; Mrs. Chapman; Mrs. M. Clarke, 3, 67, 68, 76, 82, 83, 129, 146, 157, 166; Mr. D. Craig, 144; Mr. J. Crocker, 6, 34, 65, 92, 100, 101, 107, 109, 127, 149, 161; Mr. and Mrs. J. Green; Mrs. Grinham; Mr. R. Hales, 69a; Miss J. Hardy; the late Mr. A. Hearn, 9, 124; Miss W. Heath; Henley on Thames Scout group, 152; *Henley Standard*, copies from published issues: 94 (loaned by J. W. Timms), 108 (loaned by Dr. H. Scott), 115 (lender not named), 141 (loaned by G. Turton Green), 174 (lender not named); Mrs. J. Henson, 143; Mr. Hewett; Miss Hilditch; Mrs. I. Holton, 138; Mr. J. Holton; Mr. K. M. Horswell, 79, 114, 125, 142, 162; Mr. M. Jones, 87; Mr. M. Lawlor, 69; Mrs. W. Lester; Mr. and Mrs. V. Mellett, 22, 66, 74, 75, 80, 98, 137, 154, 160; Oxfordshire County Council, Education Department, 164, 165, 167-70; Oxfordshire County Council, Department of Leisure and Arts, Library Service, 4, 5, 11, 17, 19-21, 24-6, 28-30, 40, 42, 44, 50-2, 55-7, 72, 73, 77, 78, 95, 96, 99, 117-20, 130, 136, 158 and the endpapers; Mr. and Mrs. D. Painter; Mrs. P. Perrin; Miss D. Pither, 12, 38, 81, 84, 85, 91, 148, 150; Mrs. H. K. Read; the late Mr. J. P. Read, 10, 33, 43, 54, 93, 122; the late Mr. W. G. Reeves, his collection made 1881-1936 reproduced by permission of his daughter, Miss S. Reeves, 13, 31, 41, 60, 97, 111, 112, 128, 163; Simmons & Sons, 14-16, 102-6, 121, 132; Mr. A. E. Smith; Stuart Turner Ltd., 64; Mr. N. Topsom, 37, 49, 59, 113, 123, 140, 151, 153; Mr. R. Wilson, 62, 133, 156, 172.

Pictures supplied by the authors: Mrs. A. Cottingham, 45, 46, 48, 53, 126; Mrs. H. Fisher, 7, 8, 18, 23, 27, 32, 35, 36, 39, 47, 58, 61, 63, 70, 71, 86, 110, 116, 135, 147, 159, 175.

The authors are most grateful to Simmons and Sons for allowing them access to their files of auction catalogues, from which all the auction quotations and information have been taken; to Henley and Oxford Libraries and the *Henley Standard* for access to their materials and facilities; to Tony Smith for making copies of a number of postcards; and to the people and firms in Henley who, without exception, have been unfailingly helpful and generous. Illustrations 45, 46, 48, 50, 53, 57 and 123 are some of a series of drawings and engravings made by J. Buckler, 1825-7.

Introduction

The town of Henley on Thames is believed to have been founded in the 12th century. The earliest documents concerning property in the town date mainly from the beginning of the 13th century, though there is a document of *c*.1174 which mentions property in Henley belonging to the king.

There have been finds of Roman objects in the town centre, but they are such as to suggest a single building or even a passing Romano-British subject, rather than a town or a hamlet. Saxon finds, such as swords from the river, were probably also owned by travellers, though again there might have been a farm or homestead in the area.

The shape of the town within the old boundaries indicates that Henley was a planned town. It has a regularity about it, and consists of four roads, Bell Lane, New Street, Hart Street and Friday Street, all leading to the river off the main north-south road, now Bell Street and Duke Street. (Bell Lane no longer reaches the river; it is now a cul-de-sac.) The most important of the four roads, Hart Street, or the High Street as it was once known, spreads out into the Market Place having crossed the north-south road.

The town boundary ran from the river up the centre of Friday Street, branched across from the bottom of Grays Road to the Market Place, looped around the top end of the market across what were fields, round where the hospital, once the workhouse, now stands, and then went diagonally across the main north-south road, to go down the centre of Bell Lane and so back to the river. The position of this boundary as it crosses the road to Bell Lane can be seen by the place at which, on the western side of the road, Bell Street becomes Northfield End.

A main east-west route through Henley does not seem to have been included when it was first planned. It appears to have been built as a river port, a market centre and a stop on the north-south road. Standing in the centre of the Market Place, on the town hall steps, it is not possible to see the bridge. The road leads to the church, an indication that the street plan was devised before a bridge was built. There may possibly have been a ford at the end of New Street or Bell Lane.

The present bridge, which is reached by a curve in the road round the church at the east end of Hart Street, was completed in 1786. It was situated on the north side of the previous bridge, which was then demolished. At the time of the construction of the new bridge, the road leading to it was actually staightened and widened, taking in part of the churchyard, so the road to the old bridge must have been even more curved and narrower.

The old bridge had been collapsing for years; it suffered from floods and storms, and had never recovered from damage done in the Civil War. Documentation of the old bridge goes back to *c*.1223-5, when an order was made that the Warden and Bridgemen of the town should be allowed to take wood from Windsor Forest to repair the bridge. Windsor Forest in 1225 included Remenham and Wargrave.[1] This document, though proving the existence of the bridge, does not indicate when it might have been built. It was therefore an important discovery when, in 1984, an arch of the old bridge was found. Work had begun on the construction of the new headquarters of Henley Royal Regatta, at the southeast end of the bridge. The previous building, the *Carpenter's Arms*, was removed and the old bridge arch was found between it and the present bridge. The arch was made of shuttered flint, with a double exterior arch faced with Barnack stone. The construction of the arch and the tooling on the stones indicate a date of *c*.1170.

Assuming that the town predated the bridge, it now seems likely that the town dates from the first half of the 12th century, possibly from the reign of Henry I, instead of about 1170 as previously believed. Furthermore, a document called the Cartulary of Missenden, signed *c*.1135-50 by King Stephen at Henley, might have been signed at Henley on Thames.

On modern maps of the town it is still possible to see the burgage plots on both sides of Hart Street, in parts of the Market Place and on the north side of New Street. Their presence is another indication that Henley was a planned medieval town. Burgage plots are long narrow strips of land which were leased to the burghers, usually the town's more successful businessmen and tradesmen. The narrow side of the strips lined the main streets; houses were built along the streets, filling the whole width of a plot but often designed with a passage through to yards or gardens behind.

It is possible that Henley, perhaps begun in the first half of the 12th century, was originally planned to have a main central street, now Hart Street and the Market Place, and that Friday Street and New Street were designed as back streets. The properties on the north side of Friday Street and the south side of New Street are smaller than the burgage plots, and were obviously for poorer shopkeepers and traders.

The name New Street suggests that it may have been an addition to the original design. Perhaps the town prospered so quickly that more burgage plots were needed. As a result, New Street may have been added as a main street, with extra plots on its north side. The street was already called New Street in the 13th century. There are five documents, undated but thought to be 13th-century, which record the granting of leases to properties in New Street.[2] There is also a land grant of 1307, and leases of property in 1348 and 1349.

A land boundary known as Grymes Ditch, thought to date from the Iron Age, is visible near Wallingford and continues to Huntercombe as a still fairly massive earthwork. After that it becomes indistinct, but John Crocker, a local historian, has said that it continues towards Henley through Highmoor and Lambridge Woods, and then down the centre of New Street to the river. Whether this continuation is the same ditch or dyke as the one near Wallingford is uncertain, but some earthwork, called Grymes Ditch or Dyke, *was* known in Henley. A document thought to be 13th-century mentions Grymesdyke as a boundary to land in Henley. 'Walt Bonedone to Henr Watenger. Grant of land outside his curtilage and extending to Grymesdyke, at a rent'.[3] There are further references in deeds of the 15th century. If Grymes Ditch or some other boundary came down New Street, perhaps it was originally planned as the northern boundary of the town.

The land between New Street and Bell Lane known as Countess Garden was said in 1313 to have been the site of the Manor of Henley with a garden adjacent. Countess Garden is thought to have been named after the Countess of Cornwall, widow of Edmund, Earl of Cornwall, who held the Manor of Henley in 1301. The Manor of Henley was part of the Manor of Bensington, now Benson, and was a royal demesne which included the 'hamlets of Henlee, Netelbedd, Huntercumbe, Wyfaude, Prestcromarsh, Wardburgh, Silinford and Hupholscumbe'. In 1381 it was said of Henley Manor that 'the site of the manor is of no worth, because the whole is spoiled and delapidated'.[4]

The river has always been of great importance to Henley. Throughout the medieval period and into the 17th and 18th centuries one of the most prolific trades was that of the bargemen, and the companion trade of boat-building. Henley was not only a market, but also a collecting point for all manner of goods going down river to London and elsewhere – products such as timber, wool, malt and grain. Henley's second main industry was malting and its offshoot, the brewing of beer. Much of the malt was shipped down river, but enough remained to support several breweries in the town. There is now only one brewery, Brakspear's in New Street, and malting no longer takes place in Henley.

The fortunes of the town have fluctuated, often as a result of outside influences. In the Civil War Henley was neither for the Royalists nor the Parliamentarians; the town seems to have been divided, some for one side and some for the other. At times during the war the Royalists held the town; Prince Rupert is said to have had his headquarters at the *Bell Inn* in Northfield End (later the Grammar School, see Plate 110, and now private houses). While there, Prince Rupert is said to have had a spy hanged on a tree outside the inn; the supposed remains of the tree are known as Rupert's Elm. The only fighting recorded in Henley was called the Battle of Duck Street, now Duke Street. The Parliamentarians were in the town and had a gun placed at the crossroads, facing down Duke Street. The Royalists approached from Reading, but were unsuccessful in their attempt to take the town. Many were wounded; six soldiers are recorded as being buried in the churchyard immediately after the battle, and three others a week or so later, presumably dying of wounds. Neither their names nor their allegiances are recorded.

The improvements made to the roads in the 18th century meant that people and goods started moving by road in preference to the river. This caused a slackening of the river trade, but Henley was able to continue thriving on the coaching and wagon traffic which passed through the town. Henley was a convenient stopping place and not only the inns but the whole town benefited. In 1830 coaches travelled daily to and from London, Oxford, Faringdon, Stroud, Cheltenham, Gloucester, Shrewsbury, Worcester and Holyhead.

All this activity abruptly came to an end with the advent of the railways. In the 1840s the Great Western Railway had stops at Twyford and Reading, and in 1857 a branch line to Henley. Henley was no longer on a major route, and for a time suffered a slump. Towards the end of the 19th century it began to revive as it became a holiday town and later a commuter town.

It was during this period that the Henley Royal Regatta assumed importance. The Regatta began in 1839, after some races in previous years had proved popular. It became the Royal Regatta in 1851, when Prince Albert became its patron. The Regatta takes place every year, nowadays during the 27th week of the year, usually the first week of July. It has become a five-day event, with rowing crews from all over the world taking part. The course is 1 mile 550 yards long, starting downstream just beyond Temple Island and finishing just past where Bell Lane used to go down to the river.

The photographs and drawings in this book show Henley as it was during this same period, the second half of the 19th century and up to the end of the First World War. Some pictures of the town show signs of poverty, while others show reviving prosperity. Certainly the Regatta and the attendant popularity of the river for leisure activities did much to change the fortunes of Henley. It became a desirable place to visit and to live, and the town prospered accordingly.

Professional photography in Henley seems to have started in the late 1850s. The marriage register of St Mary's, Henley, shows that on 8 November 1859 the marriage took place of Jules Nicholaus Guggenheim, photographer, of this parish, bachelor, aged 39, to Elizabeth Walklett, spinster of this parish, aged 29. The fathers were Joseph Guggenheim, manufacturer, and George Walklett, painter. In street directories[5] of 1863 and 1867 Jules Guggenheim is listed as a photographer in the Market Place.

Street directories also provide the names of other photographers in the town. By 1876 there were three photographers, George Lane at Northfield End, and Harry and Tom Marsh in Hart Street. The Marsh brothers continued to work until at least 1904, but George Lane is not mentioned as a photographer after 1876, being described as a wood turner in 1877.

In 1883 Charles Edmund and Frederick Johnson, who had been carvers and gilders, had taken up photography and continued as photographers until 1924 in Duke Street. Between 1891 and 1895 William Marshall started work in Bell Street but by 1898 had moved to Duke Street and then in 1907 to Hart Street, taking over the Marsh brothers' premises at 31 Hart Street. William Marshall is known to have taken the sequence of flood pictures in 1894 (see plates 7, 8, 9, 123 and 124).

In 1907 Arthur Edward Perrin started as a photographer and shopkeeper in numbers 13 and 15 Friday Street, but by 1908 had given up the shop at number 13, and until 1922-3 is listed as a photographer at 15 Friday Street. Thomas Pratt Barlow and Arthur Shurvell appear in 1908 as photographers in Reading Road. Barlow continued as a photographer, moving by 1915 to Duke Street. Meanwhile, Arthur Shurvell stayed in Reading Road as a picture-frame maker. George Bushell, whose photographic shop was until recently at 37 Hart Street, is first mentioned in a directory of 1924. The shop is now Vic Oddens Photographic Ltd.

Street directory entries are invaluable for a study of shops in a town, but they have a serious limitation; though they give a date for existing businesses, they do not give the date when a business began or ended. A researcher is limited by the availability and frequency of the directories. For instance, the Marsh brothers ceased trading between 1904 and 1907, these being the dates of the directories available. Again, Guggenheim could have been working in the Market Place at any time between 1854 and 1863, as there is no intervening directory; he is not listed in 1854 but appears in the 1863 directory. The probability is that he was there in 1859, that being the date of his marriage and his claim to be 'of this parish'. It could be that he was responsible for early photographs such as plates 59 and 93.

Although photography today is regarded as an art form, much early work remains anonymous. Portrait photographers often stamped the backs of the pictures with their names and trade marks, but the identity of the photographer of views and landscapes is often unknown.

Whether or not we can identify photographers, we can still appreciate their work. Not only were they intent on recording events or places with much care and artistry, but they were also highly skilled technicians, when one considers the equipment with which they achieved their results. As we quickly snap away with our modern cameras, we should pay tribute to the fine results achieved by early photographers.

1. Hatherly, J. M. & Cantor, L. M., 'The Medieval Parks of Berkshire', *Berks Archaeological Journal*, Vol. 70 (1979-80), pp. 67 & 82.

2. Hughes, M. W., 'List of the Archives of the Borough of Henley on Thames' (1928-30), Hughes Nos. 732, 749, 734, 733 & 731. (Archives listed by Hughes were then in the Bodleian Library, where they were accorded an Ancient Documents, or A.D., number; they are now in the Oxford County Record Office. The above documents are numbered A.D. 3-7.)

3. Hughes, M. W., 'List of Archives' No. 522, A.D. 8.

4. Burn, J. S., *History of Henley* (1861), pp. 228-35.

The Plates

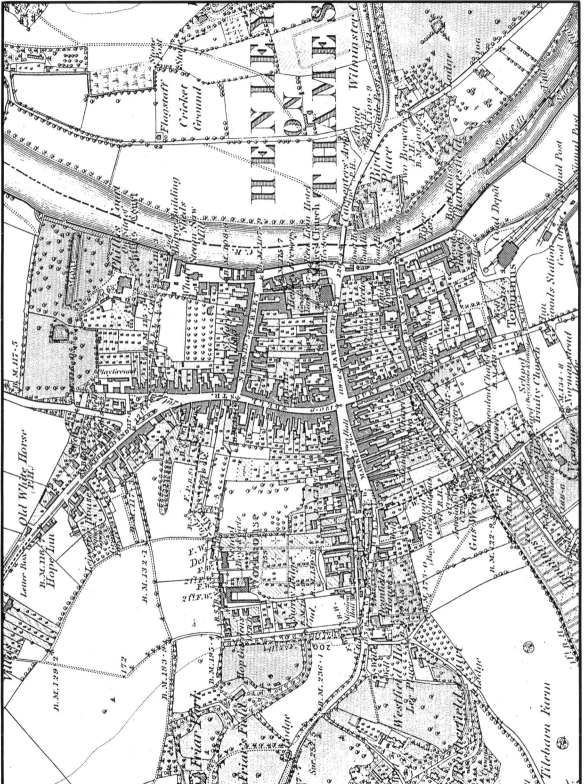

1. Ordnance Survey map, 1884.

2. A working horse being led along the towpath at Henley. In the middle distance a houseboat is manoeuvring, while a barge lies in front of the bridge. At this time, about 1890, the river was used for both work and amusement. On the left is the *Royal Hotel* (*see* plates 127-8).

3. Flooding used to be a frequent hazard but is now rare, thanks to the introduction of improved systems of controlling the water-flow. In this picture, *c.*1903, flooding can be seen through the arches of the bridge as well as at Thames side.

4.   Looking across Henley bridge to a much more open view of Remenham than today. The photograph was probably taken *c.*1870 as the toll was abolished and the removal of the toll-gate (seen in the centre of this view) was ordered by the Bridge Commissioners in 1873. The right-hand side of the *Carpenter's Arms*, later obscured by a two-storey boathouse, is here shown. The bridge was built in 1786.

5.   A similar view, dated *c.*1895. By this time a boathouse had been built in front of the *Carpenter's Arms*. When both were demolished in 1984 an arch of the earlier bridge, dated to *c.*1170, was found between the front of the *Carpenter's Arms* and the facing wall at the bridge end. The early bridge was alongside the present one. The site is now the regatta headquarters.

6. Today it is almost impossible to cross over where the young man is sitting with his wheelbarrow, *c.*1900. Beyond the *Carpenter's Arms* (extreme right) stands Bridge Cottage, later Thames Bridge House, the core of which is two much-altered cottages. The white house in the distance is the *Angel* or *Little Angel* in Remenham.

7.   The *Henley Standard* reported of the 1894 flood that 'the *Two Brewers* was inundated, the water being nearly up to the counter, and the cottagers in the Wargrave Road were in a terrible plight, being confined to the upper rooms, provisions being carried to them in boats ...'

8.   Across the road from the *Two Brewers*, the *Angel* in Remenham was also flooded in 1894. In 1751 it is said that Mary Blandy fled here, pursued by a mob when about to be arrested for the murder of her father (*see* plate 53). The landlady took pity on her and sheltered her until the carriage sent from Oxford arrived.

9. In 1894 the *Henley Standard* reported 'The flood water is rushing down the river with great velocity ... rose nearly a foot last night and is still rising ... Lion Meadows was one vast lake of water, the top of the gate leading to the meadows being only just visible. The force of the current afterwards swept the gate away ...'.

10. The previous Henley bridge was said to have been 'carried away by a flood' in 1774. In 1816 a surveyor's report suggested that the pier nearest the Oxfordshire bank of the present bridge had 'settled', causing a depression in the parapet and cornice. Regular examinations and repairs have been carried out over the years. Diving operations are shown in this view of January 1907.

11. Looking back to Henley around 1887. Following the abolition of the toll in 1873, the toll-gate was removed and the toll-collector's cottage demolished. A large house euphemistically called Toll Gate Cottage was built on the site; it was in its turn sold in 1963 and demolished.

12.   'These soldiers passed through Henley 14th September 1909' is written on the back of this postcard, collected at the time by a young military enthusiast.

3. One of a series of walking contests from Twyford railway bridge to Henley town hall in 1904. Ernest John Clegg, licensee of the *Angel on the Bridge*, is here shown passing the *Angel* at a good pace on his second walk of the day, when he took 58 minutes 45 seconds to complete the course; a distance of about 5¼ miles.

4. The *Red Lion Hotel* from across the bridge at the time of its auction in 1897. One of the best-known of old Henley coaching inns, it stands in an unrivalled position at the foot of the bridge overlooking the river. The *Red Lion* claims a long list of famous patrons, including some British and foreign royalty.

15. 'No longer an old world coaching inn, but a fashionable hotel', states the *Daily Telegraph* reporting on the modernisation and improved facilities of the *Red Lion* prior to the 1897 auction. The catalogue described a porch 'leading by folding doors to a pretty vestibule and thence by similar doors to the Central Hall 23ft by 18ft lighted by a domed skylight ...'

16. The billiard room of the *Red Lion* at the time of the 1897 auction. 'At the North End of the Central Hall is a magnificent Billiard room 31ft by 18ft with a lofty ceiling and extensive sky lights, an inlaid parquet floor and a perfect heating apparatus – this handsome room is of recent construction and has been tastefully decorated.'

17.   The south side of the bridge during a Regatta of the 1890s. Small boats are being offered for hire to visitors arriving by train. At the right end of the bridge is the *Carpenter's Arms*, demolished in 1984 to make way for the present Royal Regatta building.

18.   The regatta course in the early 1890s. At this period there were no booms defining the course, but piles had been introduced in 1886 in the hope that spectators would remain behind them.

19.   As the 1890s progressed, the crush became greater. Apart from those who watched from the larger and stationary houseboats lining the Buckinghamshire bank, most people were either rowing or punting. It is to be hoped that this photograph was taken between races.

20. The Grand Challenge Cup race of 1906. The cup, dating from the first Regatta of 1839, is competed for by 'amateur crews in eight-oared boats', according to the official programme. The problems with the crowds on the river had been regulated by the introduction of booms on the Buckinghamshire bank in 1899.

21. The Diamond Sculls c.1900, a competition introduced in 1844. This picture shows not only the booms and piles on the Buckinghamshire bank, but also the plank and pile revetment along the waterfront.

22.   This picture of 1887 shows Lord Camoys' yacht, aboard which were 'the Kings of Denmark and the Hellenes, the Prince and Princess of Wales, Prince Albert Victor, Prince George, the princesses Louise, Victoria and Maud of Wales, the hereditary Princess of Saxe-Meiningen, the Duke of Sparta and Prince George of Greece' (*Henley Royal Regatta* by Richard Burnell). A truly royal event.

23.   Another royal occasion in 1912, showing King George and Queen Mary in the royal barge. They arrived by train at Henley station, walked to the river and boarded the barge at Hobbs' landing stage. Later they went by barge to Greenlands, Hambleden, for lunch, as did the previous royal party in 1887. King George was present on both royal visits.

24.   On the left of this picture is one of the many houseboats which were such a feature of Regattas at the end of the 19th century. This picture is from the 1890s.

25.   A race in progress in the early 1900s. On the Buckinghamshire side spectators are behind the booms, and behind them are the array of houseboats crowded with people using their upper decks as grandstands.

26. The houseboat *Ibis* in the early 1900s. This was one of the larger boats which had become floating palaces, sparkling with lights, luxuriously furnished, often with grand pianos aboard and, as in this case, with a lesser boat adjacent for the galley and the servants. The upper decks on many of the boats could be dismantled to pass under bridges.

27. Some of the smaller houseboats 'dressed over-all'. In 1888 the Thames Conservancy introduced a system of allocation of places, but speculators tended to apply early and take the best places. This annoyed the genuine owners and dwellers on the boats who found themselves in poor positions. In 1889 there were 150 houseboats at Henley.

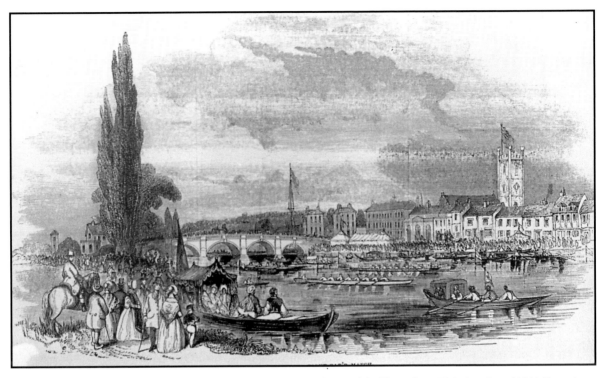

28.　Henley Regatta started in 1839 with the Grand Challenge Cup and the Town Cup. This drawing of 1844 (from the *Illustrated London News*), the year the Diamond Sculls were introduced, shows the finish just north of the bridge. Unfortunately, the crews appear to be rowing in the wrong direction.

29.　A painting of about the 1860s. Like the drawing above, it shows the finish north of the bridge, level with the steps of the *Red Lion* lawn. The first race in 1839 finished at the bridge itself, but this was considered too dangerous for future races.

30. The stands on Riverside at the finish of 'the Old Course' in 1880. In 1886 the finish was moved downstream again to Poplar Point, where it remains today, just south of Phyllis Court frontage. The aim was to create a straighter course, which was achieved in 1923 by the removal of land near the start.

31. Another view of the stand on Riverside North in the early 1880s. The buildings between Wharfe Lane and the river were then Hobbs' boatyard; in 1886 they were taken down and replaced by 'handsome boathouses with bedroom over'.

32. Lunch-time at Henley, *c.*1905. This scene is on
the bank behind the houseboats in the grounds of
Phyllis Court, nearly opposite the end of the regatta
course. In 1902 Phyllis Court was rented to the
Regatta Stewards for use as an enclosure.

33.   The river bank *c*.1880 when the boat and timber yard of Webb's Wharf extended from New Street to the grounds of Phyllis Court. This may be the site of the boat-building shed shown in plate 122.

34.   A continuation of the river bank shown above, nearer to New Street. The large shed on the right is that on the left in plate 33. On the left of this picture are three boathouses, on the right in plate 31, then commercially used. A line of houseboats are moored in front of the wharf.

35.   Phyllis Court was extensively redecorated and opened as a country club in 1906. The house was built around 1837 on the site of the ancient manor of Fillets Court, granted to John de Molyns in 1347, and was originally a moated site.

36.   A fine view of the dining hall of Phyllis Court Club with tables laid for lunch. This photograph was probably taken soon after it opened in 1906, and shows its recently refurbished interior.

37.   From about 1900 there were frequent army manoeuvres in and around Henley. This bridge-building exercise, which probably took place just before 1914, crossed the river between Lion Meadows and north of New Street.

38.   In this photograph taken during the cold winter of 1891-2 the river looks frozen all over, though the people very wisely seem to be keeping well to the edges. The small yacht with the sail is an ice-yacht; other pictures show it in full sail out on the river.

39.   The temple on Temple Island was designed by James Wyatt in 1771, when he was working at Fawley Court. It was a summer house and consisted of one room 'ornamented in a very expensive manner' in the 'Etruscan' style. (*The Freemans of Fawley and their buildings* by Geoffrey Tyack.) The regatta course starts on the right at the far end of the island.

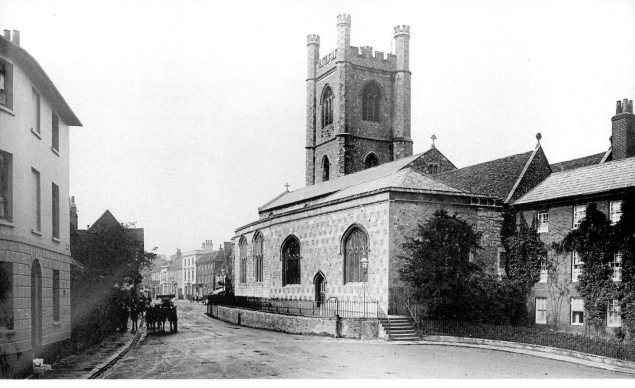

40.   The church of St Mary, from the end of the bridge, *c.*1892, showing the south aisle or Lady chapel built in the late 15th century. The church is built facing Hart Street, and this view shows the curve of the road to reach the bridge.

41.   The north side of St Mary's church before restoration. The chantry chapel of St Leonard, *c.*1460, projects on the left. The first mention of the church is in 1204, when the king gave the patronage to Americus de Harcourt. The tower was probably built in the mid-16th century, reputedly by Bishop Longland. This illustration is dated 1840.

42. Interior of the church showing the nave before restoration work was undertaken around 1850. This 1820 drawing shows box pews and upper galleries, possibly those introduced in 1818. It also shows the font and extra bench seats in the aisle.

43. The interior of St Mary's church in 1850 when restoration had raised the roof and removed the galleries and box pews. While the church was closed for restoration, services were held in what was then St Mary's Hall, now the Kenton Theatre (*see* plate 114).

44. View of the nave of St Mary's *c.*1895, showing the mural of 'The Adoration of the Lamb', painted in 1891 by the Rev. E. Geldart. The glass in the church is mostly Victorian, the east window by O'Connor dating from 1852.

45.   The Longland almshouses, endowed by Bishop Longland of Lincoln in 1547, are here pictured in their original form and position opposite the church, probably on the site of Bridge House and the garage. They were taken down in about 1830 and removed to the churchyard when the road was widened. John Longland was born in Henley in 1473.

46.   The only known drawing of the rectory demolished in about 1826. The wall on the left, now part of the rector's garage, was part of the almshouses in the view above. The rector moved to the Old Rectory on the riverside, plate 126, in 1825. This drawing, one of a series by J. Buckler, was probably made just before the demolition.

47.   Longland's almshouses were rebuilt on the west side of the churchyard in 1830. On the east side are other almshouses, ten endowed by Humphrey Newberry in 1664 and four by Mrs. Ann Messenger in 1669. All these were rebuilt in 1846 and have since been modernised and the number reduced.

48.   Longland's, the centre building, remains unchanged from 1827. The two houses to the right were taken down around 1830 to enlarge the churchyard and rebuild Longland's almshouses. The Romanesque archway on the left was removed to Fawley Court also in *c.*1830. It is not known to what building it originally belonged.

49.   A group of three old houses opposite the church, *c*.1900. The nearest of the group is alleged to be the birthplace of William Lenthall, Speaker of the Long Parliament, who refused to admit Charles I to the House of Commons in 1642. In the 18th century it housed the Henley grammar school, founded in 1604. (*See* plate 110.)

50.   J. Buckler's drawing of lower Hart Street in 1826. Note the pediment over the west door of the church and the clock on the middle window of the tower. The clock is probably the one inscribed 'Henley clock I be, Lawrance of Thame made me, 1733'.

51. Hart Street in about 1887, probably on market day, with local farmers in town – even then there were obvious parking problems, though the horses seem to have been stabled or grazed elsewhere.

52. Hart Street c.1872, a contrast to the busy scene of 1887 (plate 51). The white stuccoed house midway on the left is Blandy House, rebuilt c.1850. The brick house on the right, now Savills, was then occupied by George Riggs, maltster, and had a malthouse behind.

53. The centre building in this 1827 Buckler drawing was the scene of the poisoning of Francis Blandy, town clerk in 1751. His daughter Mary, who thought she was giving him a love potion which would make him look kindly on her lover, actually administered arsenic. She was convicted and hanged at Oxford in 1752. The house was rebuilt in about 1850.

54. An inn called the *Catharine Wheel* has been known since 1541, probably on the same site. Local papers *c.*1880-1910 carried announcements of meets of packs of foxhounds, staghounds and harriers in a wide area around Henley. A meet such as this one outside the *Catharine Wheel* in Hart Street seems to have been a rare event.

55.   The crossroads in about 1903 soon after the removal of the fountain (*see* plate 71). The large gabled building on the right, now Barclays Bank, was then J. & C. Simmonds & Co. Bank, built soon after 1896. Simmonds Bank was previously at 24 Market Place. Sidney Higgins on the left corner was a publisher of postcards.

56.   Looking up Hart Street to the old town hall in about 1890. On the extreme right is McBean Brothers, ironmongers (*see* plate 90), until recently George Bushells, the photographers.

57.   The town hall in 1826, built by William Bradshaw in 1795. It replaced an earlier guildhall nearer the crossroads, which was possibly the one 'new built' in 1487. The gabled building to the right is part of the *King's Arms*, which in 1703 was the *Queen's Arms*.

58. By *c.*1870 the Corporation required more space in its town hall and the 1795 building was extended by enclosing the open ground floor which had been used as a corn market. On the left is the *Greyhound* and beyond it the old *Victoria*. On the right is Hitchman's basket shop.

59. One of the earliest photographs taken in the 1850s, when Daniel Brown was at the *Cannon* public house; by 1861 Edward Tanner had succeeded him as publican. This also shows a side view of the 1795 town hall, and of the building immediately behind it, also used by the Corporation. On the extreme left is the *Greyhound* public house.

60. The present town hall under construction. The old town hall was dismantled in 1898 and transferred to Crazies Hill as a private house by Charles Clements, Mayor and builder. This photograph was probably taken *c*.1900.

61. The town hall as completed in 1901. The architect was Henry T. Hare and the builder McCarthy E. Fitt of Reading. The iron gates, part of the original design, were replaced by oak doors in 1909 for warmth, and 40 years later they were sold to Trinity church for £5 where they were re-erected as a war memorial.

62. To encourage the sale of war bonds, Henley held an 'Aeroplane Bank' week, 6-13 March 1918. The Mayor, Councillor R. Wilson, arranged with Major Tweedie of R.F.C. (Royal Flying Corps) that an aeroplane (probably a DH9 or DH9A) should stand in the Market Place. Inaugurating the week, Councillor Wilson 'was assisted up into the driver's place from which he addressed the assembled throng'. £21,479 7s. 6d. was subscribed during the week, as reported in the *Henley Standard*.

63. Side view of the town hall, *c*.1903-11. On the left, behind the town hall, is the road leading to King's Road, and then the *Victoria* public house which was rebuilt at the same time as the town hall, the previous *Victoria* having been demolished together with the houses and the *Greyhound* public house.

64. Goods ready for despatch to Melbourne from Stuart Turner's in 1908. The firm is now situated next door, at what was then the *Broad Gates* public house. Their world-wide trade is emphasised by other pictures showing crates ready for Vladivostock. The founder of the firm once worked at Shiplake Court, which may explain the name of the works.

65. King's Road was built at the turn of the century by Thomas Hamilton, one of the two brothers who built a large number of the late Victorian and early Edwardian terraces in Henley. There were just gardens and fields at the far end until Mount View and later Baronsmead appeared. Small patches of the distinctive yellow brick pavements still survive.

66. North side of the Market Place, *c*.1908. The corn stores, then Hawker & Son, was later for many years G. R. Cross & Son; it had previously been the post office, run by Postmaster Benjamin Palmer, which explains the position of the pillar-box, still there today.

67. The north side of the Market Place. Thomas Atkins traded here *c.*1903-10. Previously the premises were part of Plumbe's the drapers, it was later the Co-op and is now part of the site of Carpenters. In 1911 T. Atkins moved to a new building, now Spiers, which replaced the *Feathers* public house.

68. The Market Place looking down Hart Street before 1885. On the right is the *Hop Leaf* public house owned by Simmonds brewery. On the extreme left the pedimented house was then the home and surgery of Dr. Brooks, who treated the sick of Henley for about 50 years. About 1895 the house became Hales, 'the model bakery' (*see* plate 69).

69. Inside Hales & Son's bakery at 20 Market Place, *c.*1893. Thomas Hales is the boy putting a loaf in a basket, and his father, Stephen Hales, who founded the firm, is the man with the moustache, according to Mr Robert Hales, son of Thomas Hales. The ovens have now been dismantled, but the doors remain.

69a.   Advertisement on paper bags used by Hales & Son.

70.   The obelisk, removed in 1885 to Northfield End (*see* plate 86), was a milestone situated at the crossroads after the demolition of buildings known as Middle Row in the 18th century. This photograph, taken before 1883, shows the original oval shape of the upper market area with central infilling.

71. The fountain in memory of Greville Phillimore, Rector of Henley 1867-83, replaced the obelisk in 1885. In 1903 it was removed to outside the west door of the church. In 1958 a 20-foot well was found with parts of an old pump attached, which may have been the 18th-century pump alongside the obelisk.

72. Looking down Bell Street from the 'cross' in the 1890s. On the left-hand corner is Charles Monk, a linen and wool draper first mentioned in a directory of 1883. Monk & Sons continued trading until the 1950s. Note that Simpkins, linen drapers and clothiers, have extended Nos. 19 and 21 Bell Street upwards since the mid-1880s (*see* plate 73).

73. William Bunce kept the *Halfway House*, Bell Street, in the 1870s and '80s. Like many publicans he also carried on another trade: he was a fruiterer and greengrocer, though he is shown here selling rabbits. Greys brewery was bought and closed by Brakspear's in 1896, when the *Halfway House* also closed. On the left is the entrance to Gough's (Goff's) yard.

74. Bell Street, *c*.1907. Above their shopfronts the buildings on the right (east side) have changed little. On the left Richard Percy, tailor, now John Adey's, was next to Cartwrights the chemist, still trading under that name.

75.   Bell Street not long before the First World War. On the right, Eastmans the butchers remained at No. 14 for half a century before selling out to Dewhursts. Beyond are the Assembly Rooms, possibly built *c*.1770-90 as an auctioneer's and furniture showrooms. They were used as assembly rooms in the second half of the 19th century. The premises were later privately owned and available for hire.

76.   The western side of Bell Street just beyond the cinema in about 1907. George Turton Green's chemist shop was here 1899-1910, before moving to the corner of the Market Place. No. 43, Benjamin Reeves' corn merchant's shop was demolished for the Waitrose car park entrance. The imposing house beyond is still there, half Gladys Falloons and half the Franco-Belge.

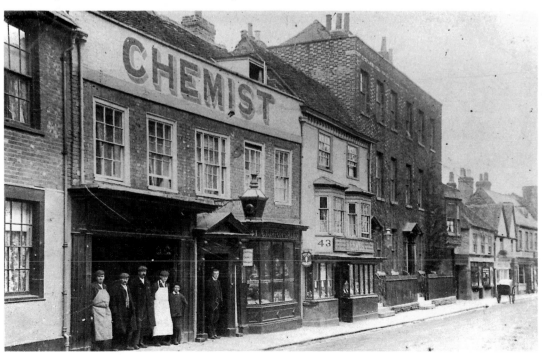

77. This photograph, taken *c*.1930, is the only known picture of the cinema before the Regal. It was established as Henley Picture Palace in June 1911, having been transformed from Henley roller skating rink. This building was demolished when the later cinema, the Regal, was built in 1937 (*see* plate 163).

78. Bell Street looking north, *c*.1895. The railings of Benjamin Reeves' residence are on the extreme left, followed by Pither, pork butcher, and a dairy – both demolished for the construction of Waitrose. Next Edward Machin, butcher, and Henry Crocker, shoemaker, were converted into Waitrose's wine department. Apart from some modern shopfronts, the right-hand side of the street is little altered.

Alfred Pither, 49 Bell Street. 'Porkman, Ham
Bacon Curer, Provision Merchant, maker of the
celebrated Henley Sausages as sent by parcel post
to all parts of the country; the Noted Pork Pie
Establishment ...' claims a 1906 advertisement in
the Henley Borough Guide. The left-hand
passageway still exists, widened to pass under the
former Reeves' residence bay window. Pither also
traded in Reading Road.

Presumably a Christmas-time display:
Edward Machin and his staff show off their wares,
including prize and commended carcases. The
display appears to dwarf Henry Crocker's
shoemaker's premises next door, but he would not
have minded as he was related by marriage to the
Machins. Between 1903 and 1935 three members of
the Machin family operated butchery businesses in
the town (see also plate 78).

81. Bell Street under snow, 25 April 1908. On 1 May the *Henley Standard* reported '... by Sunday morning there was over a foot of snow ... some of the Reading carriers had to leave their vans behind them and make their way home by train. The snow-plough and a gang of men were out early on Sunday morning, and by Church time all the crossings had been cleared ...'.

82. The *Bull Inn*, on the right of this photograph of Bell Street, advertised in 1908 in the Oxford and District Trade Directory 'horses and carriages of every description let on hire; carriages meet all trains; motor garage for 200 cars; stabling for 250 horses ...'. The *Bull* was the starting point for many of the carriers going north and east of Henley.

83. Looking south-east up Bell Street, *c.*1913. The *Bear* public house, a carter's inn, is mentioned in the 17th century. It was closed and converted into shops in 1986. Next door but one, the canopy belonging to O'Hara & Lee, butchers, is still in place along with the hooks for hanging carcases.

84. It is said that milk was delivered by oxcart belonging to Leonard Noble of Harpsden Court Farm. This photograph of *c.*1911 shows the cart passing across the old town boundary where Bell Street changes to Northfield End. The shop, at this time belonging to baker, Alfred Fowler, had been a baker's since at least the 1790s (*see* plate 111).

85. A group of soldiers resting at Northfield End in 1913. Northfield House on the left, and the large white building beyond, recently a hotel and now a restaurant, were both residential. The King's Road now runs between them, where the garden gates are in this picture.

86. Northfield End looking north, *c.*1917. The nearest group of buildings on the left are still recognisable. Behind the wagons stood Drewett's, carriage builders and motor works, now demolished and the site of Northfield Court. The obelisk on the corner of Marlow Road was moved from the town centre in 1885 (*see* plate 70).

87. John Drewett took over the *White Horse and Star* from Thomas Marlow in about 1844, having married into the Marlow family. Working as a wheelwright, he established the coach-building business, later motor works. His widow died in 1890, the public house closed in 1892 and his son concentrated on coach-building, living in the old inn to the left of the works.

ESTABLISHED 1849.

*The Royal Electric Carriage
and Motor Works.*

T.M.Drewett

Carriage Builder,

Motor Works, =

NORTHFIELD END,

HENLEY-ON-THAMES.

Carriages Fitted with Electric Light, India Rubber
Tyres, Mats, Blocks, etc.
Motor Cars Repaired & Painted. Batteries Charged.
Tyres Vulcanized. Michelin Tyres. Petrol, etc.
CARS FOR HIRE. Garage for 150 Cars.

*Your favours and recommendations are most
respectfully solicited.*

ESTABLISHED 1807.

McBean Brothers,

HART STREET (*Near the Church*),

HENLEY-ON-THAMES.

Manufacturing General and

Furnishing Ironmongers.

JONES'S PATENT
Nº 3928

CLOSED   OPEN

Hathaly lattice steps,
compact and light.

Green's patent lawn mower,
best in market.

Sanitary and Hot Water Engineers, Electrical Bell Hangers and
Coppersmiths, Braziers and General Metal Workers.

KNIFE MACHINES AND MINCERS, by the Best Makers.

BEST SHEFFIELD CUTLERY, TABLE AND DESSERT
KNIVES, MEAT AND GAME CARVERS, STEELS, RAZORS,
POCKET KNIVES, SCISSORS, BRITISH PLATE AND ELECTRO
PLATE.

CHINA AND GLASS OF EVERY DESCRIPTION.

Agents for every description of Agricultural Implements, &c., at
Makers Prices. Detailed Catalogues on application.

AGENT FOR THE NORTHERN ASSURANCE COMPANY.

HICKMAN AND KINCH,

(Members of the Pharmaceutical Society,)

Dispensing Chemists and Druggists,

PRINTERS, BOOKSELLERS & STATIONERS

HENLEY-ON-THAMES;

AGENTS FOR

TWINING'S GENUINE TEAS;

CHOCOLATE, COCOA, &c.

Fancy Snuffs, & Cigars.

Good strong Congou	5	0
Fine ditto ditto	5	4
Superior ditto	6	0
Good Souchong	7	0
Superior strong ditto	8	0
Good Twankay green	5	4
Hyson	6	0
Fine ditto	8	0
Superior fine ditto	10	0
Finest Gunpowder	10	0
Best Plantation Coffee	2	6
Twining's Cocoa	2	0
——————Compressed	1	6
——————Nibs	1	6
——————Chocolate Powder	3	0
——————Paste	3	0
Best Plain Chocolate	4	0

The smallest quantity sold is an ounce, and every
Packet is labelled "TWININGS GENUINE TEAS."

Stamps, Stationery, and Patent Medicines.
Psalms and Hymn, sung at Henley Church, Price 1s.

---

88. (*above left*) Drewett's motor works (*see* facing
page), from the 1906 Henley Borough Guide.

89. (*left*) Hickman and Kinch, from an 1838
Guide.

90. (*above*) An 1896 advertisement for McBean
Brothers (*see* plate 56).

91. The Assenden Spring flooding Northfield End in 1916. This intermittent stream was channelled along the roadside until shortly before Oxford Lodge, the large white house, from where it was piped underground to the river near Phyllis Court. On the left Drewett's garage and the cottages beyond were later demolished. Badgemore Lane is by the pedestrians.

92. The Assenden Spring flowing strongly in about 1916 but still within the confines of the culvert, which was not very deep. On the left is Leicester House, now with its gardens the site of Leicester Close. The white house on the right is the old *Old White Horse* and in front of it is Lainton or Lanton Terrace/Place.

93. Leicester House in the 1860s with the Quaker meeting house beyond. The man was recognised in 1950 by Mr. T. H. Moss as one of his uncles, who lost a leg when falling out of one of the Fairmile trees while bird-nesting. The houses on the right had obviously been demolished before 1902 (*see* plate 96).

94. The Friends' meeting house, Northfield End, prior to 1894 when all but the left-hand part was demolished. This was probably the meeting house used by the Quakers since 1668. A new meeting house was built on the site of the two smaller cottages in 1896. The old burial ground behind still exists although it is no longer used.

95.   The workforce of John Moss, agricultural machinist, in their yard which was next to Leicester House and the two houses, later demolished, shown in plate 93. The beerhouse behind is probably *The Two Magpies*, run by George Dunn in the 1840s and '50s. The census of 1851 describes it as a beerhouse and lodgings. This picture was probably taken in the 1850s.

96.   Leicester House displaying the Leander flag in about 1902. John Frederick Cooper, occupant at that time, was town clerk and also secretary to the Henley Regatta Stewards. In all probability a Leander crew was staying at the house.

97. The old *Traveller's Rest* used to stand at the far end of the Fairmile, where the roads to Oxford and Watlington divide. A larger public house (below) was built immediately behind it in about 1900. This picture of c.1899 shows on the right the roof of the *Red Cross* or *Assenden Cross* soon to be converted to a private house.

98. The replacement *Traveller's Rest* built c.1900. It was closed at the beginning of 1938 and demolished about a year later for road widening. The narrow chalk road to Bix and Nettlebed can be seen to the left, and on the extreme left is the entrance to the municipal cemetery.

99. Looking towards Henley from the further end of the Fairmile, *c*.1893. The tall Oxford Villas can be seen at the far end. The avenue of elms shown here was planted by Sir Thomas Stapleton in 1751; sadly they had to be felled in 1953. The shallow channel of the Assenden Spring is dry.

100. The beginning of the Fairmile looking towards the town in about 1914. Oxford Cottages, the row on the left, are easily recognisable. The road is here little more than a cart track; animals used to graze by the roadside.

101. Looking at Oxford Villas, built in the mid-19th century, from the Mount across the Fairmile wall (*see* plate 108).
Beyond can be seen the fields and allotments, now Abraham's estate. Top left, the houses of Hop Gardens are visible. The
turret of Friar Park can be seen on the skyline on the right.

102. Friar Park was built soon after 1889 by Sir Frank Crisp, a London solicitor, on Friar Park and Friar's Field. George Harrison, one of the Beatles, now lives there. Throughout the house, friars were used as decorative motifs; moveable noses of friars switched on lights indoors, while friars' faces adorned gargoyles outside.

103. The 'Jacobean' entrance hall at Friar Park was 37 ft. high with a carved oak staircase and encircling gallery. The capitals of the pillars showed friars engaged in sleeping, dreaming, snoring, yawning and waking. A pilgrim friar welcomed visitors at the entrance and on each side were statues of two friars showing the narrow and the broad way.

104. The dining room inglenook fireplace flanked by columns supporting friars, and with statues of friars on the mantelshelf. The dining room was heavily beamed and had a richly-carved Jacobean sideboard. The wall space above an oak dado was filled by embossed and gilded leather.

105. Part of the 42-ft. double drawing room, with one of the Italian carved alabaster fireplaces. The ceiling and walls were decorated with low relief plaster work and painted panels. The window at the end led to a garden alcove with steps to the famous caves and rock gardens.

106. The 62 acres of gardens at Friar Park were fantastically designed. A rock garden with every known species of rockplant contained a miniature Matterhorn. Water features with bridges, stepping stones and watercaves abounded. There were Japanese. topiary, sun-dial and medieval gardens. This photograph shows the Gnomes' Cave or Grotto, one of many such caves. (Nos. 102-106 are as described in the auction catalogue of 1919.)

107. Northfield End looking towards the obelisk in the distance. On the left the *Old White Horse* was rebuilt further back from the road in 1938. On the extreme right is Portland Cottage. In the middle distance the three-storey Leicester House stands out behind the conifers in the garden. The culvert for the Assenden Spring appears to be dry.

108. The former *Old White Horse* at Northfield End, *c.*1905. The brick and flint wall, built in 1804 by Strickland Freeman as a boundary wall of the Fawley Court estate, can be seen behind the public house. The *Old White Horse* was later rebuilt further back from the road, causing a break in the wall.

109. The delivery trap of William Norris at Northfield End. Its back is to the Fairmile and the Marlow Road heads towards the top left. Norris was a baker and also licensee of the *Red Cow* beerhouse in West Hill. The building on the left, the first house after the road junction, used to be Northfield End post office.

110. Henley Grammar School (*see* plate 49), whose foundation can be traced back to 1604, occupied part of the premises of the *Bell Inn* from *c*.1840 until 1928. The *Bell* was an important coaching inn, which probably gave its name to Bell Street. In front is the elm tree from which Prince Rupert reputedly hanged a Parliamentary spy in 1643.

111. A carrier's cart, possibly belonging to T. Palmer of Benson, and the delivery cart of Miss Emma Gill, a baker at 95 Bell Street *c*.1883-1907, outside Miss Gill's premises in about 1900. Later the bakery was that of Alfred Fowler (*see* plate 84).

112. New Street decorated with flags to celebrate the Relief of Mafeking in 1900. The shop on the north-west corner was Alfred Austin & Co., grocers.

113. New Street in about 1905. The house on the right is one of the older houses in Henley, possibly 15th-century. Beyond are five cottages called Barnaby Groat Cottages. Built in 1788, they replaced two houses given to the town in 1582. Their rents raised money for the Barnaby Groat charity.

114.   New Street before the First World War. On the left, just beyond the white gabled house, is the brick façade of the Henley theatre, now called the Kenton. Built as a theatre in 1805, it was used as a church hall and a school until the 1920s. It is now once more a theatre.

115.   The eastern end of New Street before Brakspear's Mineral Water Manufactory was built in 1897. The cottages on the immediate right are still there, now known as Tudor and Ann Boleyn Cottages. The archway on the left led into a yard where a new malthouse was built by Brakspear's in 1899.

116. A view of the bridge from the bottom of New Street in 1820. This was still the heyday of the barge trade, when Henley was a river port; one of the barges is tied up at the riverside.

117. The great flood of 1894 at the bottom of New Street. The flood can be seen stretching across Lion Meadow in the distance, now known as Regatta Meadows.

118. A peaceful scene at the public slipway at the bottom of New Street in 1898. Hobbs & Sons' boat business occupies the boathouses on the right. In the far distance the tower and turrets of Friar Park can be seen (*see* plates 102-6).

119.   A broad sweep of the riverside in about 1890. Mr. Shepherd's boat-building business at the *Red Lion* appears to be busy. *The Little White Hart*, the left-hand part of the white buildings on the waterfront, has yet to be rebuilt. The 'working' boathouses on the right were rebuilt soon after as leisure accommodation with a boathouse underneath.

120.   Waterside in the 1880s. *The Red Lion Family Hotel* was run by Mrs. Elizabeth Williams from about 1852 until her death in 1888. On the right of the picture was stabling, later rebuilt as a boathouse. Part of the Greys brewery and malthouse in Friday Street can be seen on the left.

121.   Having taken over the *Red Lion*, Mr. Tom Shepherd in 1889 converted the riverside range of stabling into 'a commodious boathouse ... on two floors'. The ground floor area was used for storing and letting boats, while upstairs was 'a first-rate boat-building room 83 ft. × 41 ft. opening by French doors on to a picturesque balcony'.

122.   A boat yard in Henley, possibly on Webb's Wharf (*see* plates 33-4). The boat business at the *Red Lion*, established 1888, was appointed boat-builder to the Sultan of Turkey and won awards at the Paris Exhibition in 1889 and Scheveninger in 1891. An order to construct 'twenty-six new boats for the Corporation of Southport' was in hand when the business was auctioned in 1897.

123. The 1894 flood was the worst for almost 100 years. As described in the *Henley Standard*, 'Mr. Harvey's and the adjoining cottage [against which the ladders stand] were flooded to a depth of several feet and the Rectory was also inundated. The roadway in front of River Terrace was submerged, the water being about 2 ft. deep'.

124. In 1894 the *Henley Standard* reported 'the rushing water broke down the railings of the *Red Lion Hotel* lawn and covered the pavement from the end of the hotel to New Street'. The *Little White Hart* was flooded with water 2 ft. deep around the bar: '... planks were fixed along the bar and many persons visited the house for the purpose of witnessing the novel sight ...'.

125. The *Little White Hart* soon after it was rebuilt, *c.*1900. Previously a small riverside beerhouse associated with those working on the river, it was the home of the Henley United Rowing Club, a club for river workers as opposed to Henley Rowing Club for amateurs and gentlemen. The rowing clubs were later combined.

126. The rectory on Riverside in 1827, soon after it had been acquired for use as the 'Rectory House' by the incumbent, the Rev. James King. The previous rectory (*see* plate 46) had stood further back from the road behind the tree and wall to the right of this rectory. The adjoining coach house was later rebuilt.

127. The *Royal Hotel* and River Terrace in *c*.1918. River Terrace was built in *c*.1866 and in 1871 was occupied by families new to the district. Most of the terrace later became lodging houses. The *Royal Hotel*, rebuilt on part of the site of the earlier *Royal Hotel* (*see* below), ceased trading in *c*.1925 and was turned into flats, though the bar in Station Road continued as a public house.

128. The river wing of the old *Royal Hotel*, opened in 1872, faced south towards Marsh Meadows and lock. It was advertised in the 1876 Harrod Directory as '... quite detached ... 14 acres ... croquet lawn and beautifully laid out grounds in the Italian style with terrace walk ...'. Unsuccessful, by 1883 it was 'open during the summer season only'. Before 1872 it was Baltic House, from *c*.1864 the home of Robert Owthwaite (1804-87), Mayor and speculative builder. On the left is the garden wing of the hotel which, following the rebuilding of the river wing (*see* above), became the Convent of the Ursuline Nuns (*see* plate 133).

129. Marsh Mills on the Berkshire bank at Marsh Lock, here pictured *c*.1905, was a flour mill until at least the Second World War. It is probably the approximate site of the Domesday Book mill in Remenham parish. These buildings have been converted into flats; the boathouse on the right belonged to Marsh Mills House.

130. Marsh Mills House was originally the residence of the proprietor of the mill. A spacious house and grounds, it is today hardly visible from the river, being screened by the now mature 'clumps and beds of lovely ornamental trees, and choicest flowering shrubs' of the 1901 auction catalogue. On the left, part of the mill is also visible.

131. On the Oxfordshire bank at Marsh Lock, the extensive New Mills was probably the site of the mill in Peppard parish, mentioned in Domesday Book. In these parts all upland parishes had access to the river, Peppard's being a narrow strip, little wider than the present Peppard and Mill Lanes. New Mills was last a paper mill, production ceasing in about 1904.

132. New Mills House, 'remarkably well built of stone and approached by a tiled forecourt and fine portico entrance' at the time of its auction in 1904. Intended as the mill proprietor's house, a more recent owner was Danny la Rue. The auction catalogue noted that the water frontage included 'the mill tail water ... noted for its excellent Barbel Fishing'.

133.   The firm of Richard Wilson building Hobbs' boathouse on the riverside at the end of Station Road in about 1898. The house on the right in the background was later the Ursuline Convent, which was situated between the *Royal Hotel* and Searles boathouse (*see* plate 128 on the far left, and plate 162).

134.   The corner of Thames side and Friday Street. On the left is Baltic Cottage, said to be named after the Baltic Mercantile and Shipping Exchange. On the right the building now called the Old Granary is probably here being used for boat storage and other warehouse activities, though it was once a granary.

135. Friday Street from the river, *c.*1890. On the side of the *Anchor* are the words 'Greys Brewery Tap', denoting its position near the Greys brewery, which was bought by Brakspear's and closed in 1896. The town boundary ran down Friday Street so all properties on the left were in Rotherfield Greys.

36. Friday Street, *c.*1887. Greys brewery was behind the *Anchor* on the left; further down on the right was the ironworks, previously a tannery, and beyond it was the paper bag factory and printers, probably at this time newly built.

37. The *Anchor Hotel* in about 1905, after alterations. The lady may have been the wife of the landlord, Joseph Massie Furnival, who was at the *Anchor* from 1900 to 1928.

138.   Friday Street, *c.*1890. On the right was the *Black Horse*, now a private house, and next to it were the cottages later demolished for the drill hall. The tall house beyond, then part of Greys brewery, was later converted into a smaller building (*see* below).

139.   This view of Friday Street, though taken in about 1930, shows the street as it was before 1920. The building beyond the white fronted house on the left was the iron foundry, begun *c.*1869. On the right the *Black Horse* is no longer trading, the cottages are still there, but the tall building (as seen above) is now much smaller.

140.   Duke Street photographed in the 1860s, before the street was widened in about 1870 by the demolition of the entire west, or left, side. Known previously as Duck Street or Brook Street from the town ditch which flowed across its southern end, in 1642 it was the site of a Civil War battle.

141.   The *Blue Bell* or *Bell* public house, on the east corner of Duke Street and the south side of Hart Street, was closed in about 1890. The corner was rebuilt in 1894 and was for many years the premises of W. H. Smith. It now houses Foster's Menswear. The white stuccoed building on the left in Hart Street looks much the same today.

142. Duke Street, *c*.1907. W. H. Smith's was on the Hart Street/Duke Street corner from *c*.1907 to the 1960s. W. Taylor, confectioner, lasted only a short time on the opposite corner; by 1911 the premises were occupied by George Turton Green, chemist. In the far distance can be seen the projecting gable end of Southfield House (*see* plates 147 and 174).

143.   John Hawkins' glass, china and cutlery stores in Duke Street, *c*.1905. Next door at numbers 13/15 was H. Hawkins, fancy draper and furrier. John Hawkins commenced business as a grocer, china and glassware retailer in Bell Street in 1876, and the business continued in Duke Street until 1950. Queen Mary visited this emporium on several occasions.

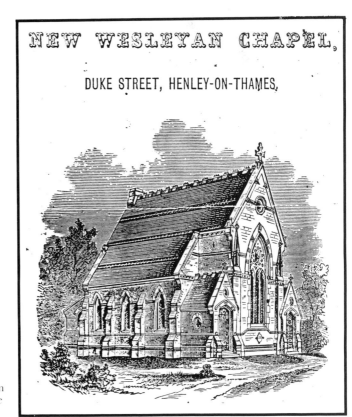

144.   The Wesleyan chapel in Duke Street was opened in 1874, with seating for 160 people, and was enlarged the following year. Wesley himself visited Henley and preached in the town. The Methodist congregation now holds services in St Mary's parish church since the chapel was closed in 1980, when the cost of its upkeep could no longer be met. It was subsequently demolished.

145.   Frederick Sheppard and before him Reuben Sheppard were bakers and grocers in Duke Street from about 1883 to 1910. A grocery business was later carried on by Self and Horswell on this site, which was recently gutted and rebuilt for 'Printworld'. Beyond, the small white building was rebuilt in the 1930s and 'Tudorised'. Across Friday Street is the post office, now Lloyd's Bank.

146. Albert Road was built in the late 1880s by William Hamilton, who intended to continue the road to connect with Norman Avenue. However, Charles Clements who was building larger houses in Norman Avenue did not want a connection to be made. He therefore built houses across the end of Albert Road while Hamilton was visiting America.

147.   Looking south along Reading Road c.1908. On the left is the late Victorian post office, now Lloyd's Bank. On the right is Southfield House, demolished to make way for the present post office which opened in 1922. Next door is the house which lately was a tobacconist's and Leaver's garage.

148.   In the early years of this century annual troop exercises took place, often in this area. Here a contingent passes along Reading Road in 1913. The new Congregational church and cottages housing the old *Three Horseshoes* and chimney sweep George Rose are visible: both signs protrude. Adjoining is the further end of Southfield House garden wall.

149.   On the right can be seen how the *Three Horseshoes* jutted into Reading Road until its demolition for road widening in 1930. The site is now the wide pavement in front of E. T. Sheppard, stonemason. Gladstone Terrace looks very different with its porches, but the parade of shops beyond has changed little.

150. The Congregational chapel, built in 1719 and enlarged in 1829, seated 500. After the new chapel (below) had been completed, the last service was held on Sunday 19 July 1908. This chapel was demolished in March/April 1909. In 1662 Rev. Brice, the rector of Henley, was expelled from his living and took some of his parishioners to worship outside Henley, thus forming the Congregationalists.

151. The Congregational church still looking very new. The first service was held there on Tuesday 21 July 1908, but the following Sunday, 25 July, a special service was held, attended by the mayor and corporation and the crews of the olympic Regatta, 'the Mayor having ascertained that most of the competitors were Protestants, the Norwegians being Lutherans'. (*This Glorious Henley* by George H. Peters.)

152.   The 1st Henley on Thames (Y.M.C.A.) Scout group assembles on Station Meadow, *c.*1911. The chimneys of the south side of Hamilton Avenue are visible and the possible forerunner of Sargeant's garage, a 'motor pit and garage', stands beside the *Wheatsheaf*'s 'Best Stables'. The Henley Scout troop was formed in 1908, one of the earliest in the country.

153.   The present *Three Horseshoes* on the corner of Harpsden Road was built by Brakspear's in 1899. However, permission to transfer the licence was only obtained when the old *Three Horseshoes* site (*see* plates 148-9) was required for road-widening, and this building was a shop until 1930. These Victorian terraces in Reading and Harpsden Roads were largely built by William Hamilton between 1890 and 1900.

154.   Harpsden Road, once Harpsden Lane, was built in the 1890s by William Hamilton, who named all his terraces. In Harpsden Road are Cleveland, Manitoba and Toronto Terraces. In the distance can be seen the *Three Horseshoes*, built in 1899 but not yet a public house (*see* above). There were no houses at this time on the left side of the road.

155. One change in the lifestyle of town-dwellers during the last hundred years has been the disappearance of the numerous small specialist businesses and shops. The proprietors and families worked very long hours for small profits. This small general store was in the front room of 28 Manitoba Terrace, Harpsden Road. The small boy with the dog was Fred Chapman.

156. Reading Road looking towards Henley in 1909. On the left the large houses, now demolished, were between St Andrew's Road and St Mark's Road. The entrance to St Mark's Road is by the light-coloured wall in the distance, and beyond are the houses between St Mark's Road and Hamilton Avenue, which still exist.

157. Station Road looking towards the railway station before the First World War. Higgs stands then, as today, on the Reading Road corner. The stretch of road was widened into a dual carriageway in 1926 by taking in the northern edge of Station Meadow. The road was built by the Great Western Railway company as access to the station and was closed every evening.

158. Henley railway station in the early part of this century. Henley was connected to the Great Western Railway network in 1857, several earlier schemes having fallen through. Public demand for a connection spurred the company into action. Originally broad gauge, the line was converted to standard gauge in 1876.

159. In the Edwardian era about 30,000 regatta visitors arrived by rail each year. Special through trains, many non-stop, were laid on from Paddington, Windsor, Didcot and Oxford; extra staff were brought from all over the Great Western Railway's network. Goods traffic was rescheduled to avoid interference with the extra trains and Henley sidings were cleared for empty carriages to await return journeys.

160. The *Imperial Hotel* as it would have been seen by passengers arriving at Henley in about 1907. The shops, with residential accommodation above, and the hotel in the middle, were completed in 1897, but some premises were not occupied until a few years later. After the opening of the *Imperial*, now the *Edwardian*, the crescent was sometimes known as Imperial Parade.

161. The original turntable was situated north of the station; thus the old line of Station Road circumnavigated it. In 1903 a new turntable was built, where Hewgate Court now stands, enabling the construction of a new straight road, with improvements to the station entrance. This photograph of about 1918 shows to the right the Y.M.C.A. hall and the Congregational church spire.

162. 'All kinds of boats for hire at the Royal and Angel stages. Awarded silver Medallion for Excellence at Construction by the Royal Naval Association of Lisbon 1904', reads the advertisement in the 1906 Henley Borough Guide which reproduced this picture. The building in Station Road, occupied by Searle's *c*.1890-*c*.1924, was more recently the Central garage.

163. The Whit Monday van horse parade outside the *Imperial* between 1898 and 1904. G. T. Savage had premises in Bell Street. In 1911 he obtained an injunction against F. Ellis for the nuisance caused by the working of an engine and dynamo for the exhibition of cinematographic pictures (*see* plate 77). The defendant claimed he would make alterations to abate the noise and vibrations.

164. The British School, 6 July 1904, on the Norman Avenue/Reading Road corner, was erected by public subscription in 1856 and was non-denominational, although closely associated with and adjacent to the Congregational church. The prospect of heavy repair bills in the changed circumstances of state education led to its closure in 1932. A small part is still identifiable as the carpet cleaners.

165. The main schoolroom of the British School, also photographed on 6 July 1904. The desk tops have been up-ended, presumably for ease of cleaning. The inkwells would probably have been distributed only when needed.

166.   Holy Trinity church opened in 1848 to care for the increasing number of souls living south of the Friday Street/Greys Lane line, the boundary of Henley parish. They were parishioners of Rotherfield Greys, whose church is 2 ½ miles up-country.

167.   Contemporary with Trinity church is the old Trinity Infants' School on Greys Hill, now a private house. Opened in 1850, by 1854 it had an average daily attendance of 50 pupils. The 1844 tithe map shows the lower half of Greys Hill already built up, including Trinity and Cromwell Cottages below the school. This photograph was taken on 7 March 1906.

168. The babies' room of Trinity Infants' School on 7 March 1906. Unfortunately the time needed to take photographs at that date has caused the children to move so their faces are blurred. The pictures on the walls appear to be more interesting than might be expected at that time. There is what appears to be a maypole in the corner.

169. The infants' room of Trinity Infants' School on Greys Hill, also photographed on 7 March 1906, with a lesson in progress. The gas pipe with its two mantles is here left bare, unlike in the other classroom (*see* above) where decorations have been suspended from it.

170. The National School was established in 1817 in New Street at the Kenton or St Mary's Hall (*see* plate 114). In 1848 a school was built between Gravel Hill and Greys Lane, now part of Henley College. This building on Gravel Hill was the girls' school built in 1879, photographed in June 1904 by the Director of Education for Oxfordshire, who also photographed the preceding pictures of schools.

171. Station Road looking towards the Reading Road in about 1907. John Bowyer, plumber and decorator, had premises on the corner of Queen's Street. The trees bordering the single carriageway remained in the middle of the dual carriageway (*see* plate 157) until the 1970s. The 'For Sale' notice appears to be at Wheatsheaf Meadow, where auctions were sometimes held.

172. The majority of the coal merchants had premises in the vicinity of the station. Dunlop's office fronted the Reading Road, with stables behind – on the extreme right – but the coalyard extended through to Queen Street, with access there. Next door at 50 Queen Street was Wakefields, later Holtons, another coal merchants. Dunlop's were in Reading Road between about 1891 and 1980.

173. Gladstone Terrace was earlier known as Chapel Row as it faced the Congregational chapel (*see* plates 149-150). Apart from the Gladstone Terrace porches, the east side of Reading Road has not changed much, only the shop fronts being different. This view emphasises how much the *Three Horseshoes*, porch and sign, just visible on the left, obstructed the thoroughfare.

174. Reading Road looking towards Duke Street, *c.*1890. On the left is Southfield House; the *Queen's Head* is just discernible, as is the west side of Duke Street. On the right, the wall and trees predate the construction of the 1895 post office (*see* plates 145 and 147), and across Friday Street stands the residence of Mr. C. S. Plumbe, where Oxford House was built in 1897.

175. Coronation celebrations in Reading Road, 1911, beside Southfield House wall (*see* plates 147 and 174). After a cannon salute and the ringing of church bells, church services and a mayoral breakfast, there was a grand procession around the town. Seen leading the parade are the mounted squad of Henley Yeomanry, then the Henley town band, a troop of Henley Yeomanry, Henley Company of Territorials and members of friendly societies and many others.

HENLEY.

176. Henley's peace celebrations took place on 19 July 1919, commencing with a reception of returned servicemen at the town hall at 11 a.m., continuing with processions, sports and entertainments at Fawley Court, and culminating with a bonfire at the Mount (*see* plate 101) at 11 p.m. Here, part of the procession passes through Duke Street.